make

pincushions

12 Darling Projects to Sew

C&T PUBLISHING

Text, photography, and artwork copyright © 2016 by C&T Publishing, Inc.

Publisher: Amy Marson

Creative Director: Gailen Runge

Editors: Joanna Burgarino and Alice Mace Nakanishi

Cover/Book Designer: April Mostek

Production Coordinator: Zinnia Heinzmann

Photography by Diane Pedersen, Christina Carty-Francis, and Nissa Brehmer, of C&T Publishing, unless otherwise noted

For further information and similar projects, see the book listed after each artist's bio.

Published by C&T Publishing, Inc., P.O. Box 1456, Lafayette, CA 94549

Contents

Log Cabin Pincushion

Alexia Marcelle Abegg

FINISHED SIZE:
6″ × 6″ × approximately 1″ thick

This little pincushion is a twist on the Log Cabin block that is embellished with rickrack.

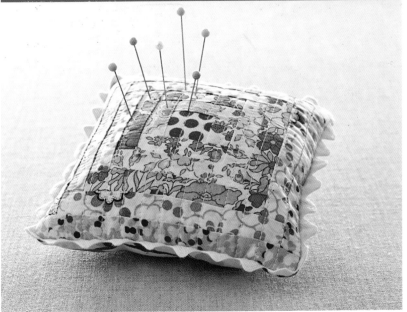

ALEXIA MARCELLE ABEGG

is an award-winning artist and designer who studied fashion and fine arts. Her experience in photography and costuming has helped her find her home in designing quilt and sewing patterns. Alexia lives in Tennessee.

WEBSITE:
alexiaabegg.squarespace.com

This project originally appeared in *Liberty Love* by Alexia Abegg, available from Stash Books.

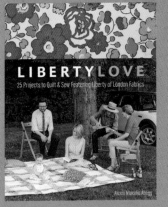

Available as an eBook only

Materials and Supplies

RED PRINT: 1½″ × 1½″ for center

VARIETY OF PRINTS: 10 strips 1″ wide (from 1½″ to 6½″ length) for logs

VARIETY OF PINK AND RED PRINTS: 10 strips 1″ wide (from 1½″ to 6½″ length)

BACKING: ¼ yard or scrap 7″ × 7″

BATTING: 7″ × 7″

RICKRACK: ¾ yard, ³⁄₈″ wide

STUFFING

Cutting

RED PRINT: Cut 1 square 1½″ × 1½″.

COTTON PRINT 1″ STRIPS: Arrange and cut the 1″-wide fabric strips according to the length shown in the block diagram.

BACKING FABRIC: Cut 1 square 6½″ × 6½″.

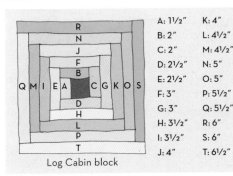

Log Cabin block

A: 1½″	K: 4″
B: 2″	L: 4½″
C: 2″	M: 4½″
D: 2½″	N: 5″
E: 2½″	O: 5″
F: 3″	P: 5½″
G: 3″	Q: 5½″
H: 3½″	R: 6″
I: 3½″	S: 6″
J: 4″	T: 6½″

Construction

Use a ¼″ seam allowance, and sew all seams with the right sides together.

TOP

1. Sew strip A to the left of the 1½″ × 1½″ center square. Press the seam away from the center square.

2. Sew strip B to the top of the unit. Press the seam away from the center square.

3. Continue sewing strips in alphabetical order until you have completed the block.

4. Layer the Log Cabin block onto the batting with the wrong side touching the batting. Press.

5. Using a straight stitch, quilt rows of stitching every ¼″–½″ across the block. Trim away any excess batting.

6. Beginning at the center of a side of the top, sew the rickrack trim in place, centering it on the ¼″ seamline. Overlap the rickrack ends and let each veer over the cut edge of the pincushion top. Backstitch over the rickrack. Trim excess.

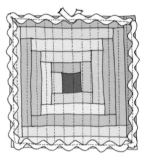

PINCUSHION

1. On the wrong side of the backing, make 2 marks on the seam allowance about 2½″ apart and centered on a side for turning right side out after sewing.

2. Pin the top and backing of the pincushion, right sides together.

3. With the bottom facing up, sew around the perimeter—begin at an opening mark, pivot at each corner, and stop when you reach the other opening mark.

4. Clip the excess seam allowance at each corner.

5. Turn the pincushion right side out.

6. Stuff until the pincushion is fairly firm.

7. Using a ladder stitch, stitch the opening of the pincushion closed.

Kaleidoscope Pincushion

Jeni Baker

FINISHED SIZE: 5″ × 5″

Most sewists can never have enough pincushions, even with five or six at the ready. For Kaleidoscope Pincushion, a Nine-Patch block was altered to become something fresh and different.

Materials and Supplies

SOLID FABRIC SCRAPS: 18 squares 2″ × 2″

BACKING FABRIC: 6″ × 6″

STUFFING

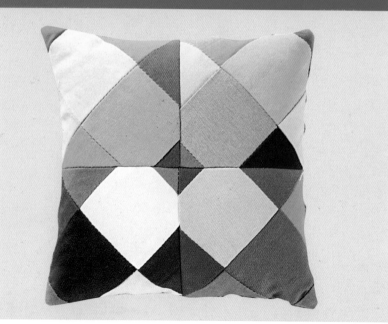

Construction

All seam allowances are ¼".

1. Arrange and sew the squares into 2 Nine-Patch blocks. Press the seams open.

2. Sew the Nine-Patch blocks, right sides together, on all 4 sides.

3. Cut the blocks diagonally twice.

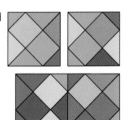

4. Open the pieces and press the seams open.

5. Arrange and sew 2 rows of 2 pieced squares each. Join the rows. Press the seams open.

6. Layer the pieced pincushion top with the 6" × 6" backing, right sides together. Trim any excess backing. Sew around all 4 sides, leaving a 1" opening along a side.

7. Turn right side out, clipping the corners and poking them out with a dull pencil. Stuff the pincushion as desired, and hand stitch the opening closed.

tip You don't have to use fiberfill to stuff your pincushions. Try sand, ground walnut shells, or emery powder to help keep your pins sharp and ready for your next project!

JENI BAKER loves to find ways to be creative every day, whether through photography, sewing, or quilting. Recently she entered the world of fabric design as a licensed designer for Art Gallery Fabrics. She also writes and publishes sewing and quilting patterns.

WEBSITE: incolororder.com

This project originally appeared in *Stitch 'n Swap* (from Stash Books), which was compiled by Jake Finch.

Boxy Pincushion

Virginia Lindsay

FINISHED SIZE:
4″ wide × 4″ high × 1½″ deep

Fabric: This pincushion features Dear Stella's fabric Do It Yourself Scissors in White and Ann Kelle's Ovals in Lime

The shape of this pincushion is practical but pretty too. It holds lots of pins and fits nicely right next to your machine.

Materials and Supplies

UPPER HALF FABRIC:
1 square 6″ × 6″

CONTRASTING LOWER HALF FABRIC:
1 square 6″ × 6″

STUFFING

COORDINATING EMBROIDERY FLOSS:
1 yard

1 BUTTON, 1″ WIDE

EMBROIDERY NEEDLE

Construction

Seam allowances are ¼″ unless otherwise noted.

1. Pin and sew together the upper and lower pieces, right sides together. Leave a 2″ gap on one side to turn the piece right side out later.

2. To make a boxed corner, pinch one corner flat so the seams line up. Pin flat and sew perpendicular to the seams ¾″ away from the tip. Trim away the excess corner fabric, leaving a ¼″ seam allowance. Repeat with the other 3 corners.

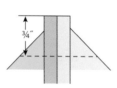

3. Turn the pincushion right side out and stuff it. Use a chopstick to get the stuffing into the corners so it looks nice and full. Hand sew the opening with a blind stitch or ladder stitch.

4. Using the embroidery floss and needle, anchor the thread by making a few back-stitches in the center of the bottom of the pincushion. Pull the thread around one side of the pincushion, down through the top at the center, and out the bottom where you first began. Repeat this step to sew around all 4 sides of the pincushion.

Hand stitch from bottom to top.

5. Bring the thread back to the top of the pincushion, and stitch the button in place at the center several times. Knot the floss and clip the end.

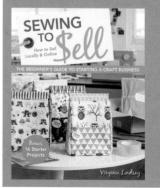

Sew Me a Pincushion

Kajsa Wikman

FINISHED SIZE:
5″ × 3″ (12.7 cm × 7.6 cm)

This is a great first free-motion stitching project. I suggest that you cut out several patches of fabric and experiment with the free-motion script. If you end up with a number of nice pieces, you can make several pincushions or maybe use the patches for a quilt. Try stitching many different words.

KAJSA WIKMAN is an artist, teacher, and blogger. She also runs a business, Syko Design, which specializes in happy, childlike appliqué designs and printed products. Kajsa lives in Helsinki, Finland.

WEBSITE: syko.fi

This project originally appeared in *Scandinavian Stitches* by Kajsa Wikman, available from Stash Books.

Materials and Supplies

NATURAL-COLORED LINEN OR COTTON: 4″ × 5″ (10.2 cm × 12.7 cm) scrap

PRINT FABRIC: 6″ × 6″ (15 cm × 15 cm) square for back

COTTON PRINT: 3 scraps for small patches

THREAD: Black 30-weight

STUFFING

ERASABLE FABRIC PEN OR PENCIL

RIBBON: 3″ (7.6 cm) length

 tip If you want a key ring instead of a pincushion, you can make a slightly smaller pillow and add a ring or natural twine to the short side.

Cutting

LINEN: Cut 1 piece 3½″ × 4½″ (8.9 cm × 11.4 cm) for front.

PRINT: Cut 1 piece 3½″ × 5½″ (8.9 cm × 14 cm) for back.

PRINT SCRAPS: Cut 3 squares 1½″ × 1½″ (3.8 cm × 3.8 cm).

tip I suggest that you cut a number of pieces from the linen if you want to practice free-motion stitching. If you prefer to work with a larger piece of fabric that is easier to handle, mark the sewing area on the linen fabric with a pen, and cut it out when you have finished stitching the text.

Construction

Seam allowances are ¼" (6 mm) unless otherwise noted.

1. Set your sewing machine for free-motion stitching: lower the feed dogs, and attach the darning foot. Thread the machine with black thread.

2. Draw the script on the linen patches with an erasable fabric pen or pencil. I suggest that you use your own handwriting and try a variety of words to practice and find your own writing style.

3. Start stitching, keeping the fabric flat with your hands while slowly

moving it forward. Stop and breathe! Then go on.

4. Using the project photo as a guide, sew the 3 small squares together. Press. Sew them to the linen patch. Press.

5. Place the unit from Step 4 right sides together with the backing piece. Fold the ribbon in half, and baste along the side seam, with the fold on the inside. Stitch around the edges, leaving an opening.

6. Turn the piece right side out, and stuff firmly. You will need a lot of stuffing for a pincushion; you don't want the needles to come through the cushion.

7. Stitch the gap closed by hand.

Start a new sewing project using your pincushion!

Little Cabin Pincushion

Bari J. Ackerman

FINISHED SIZE:
4½" w × 3" h × 6" d

This neat little cabin is a fun addition to your sewing room. It will give you a pretty spot for your pins, and it has a place to store your sewing needles so they don't end up buried somewhere deep in the carpet (ahem... like in my studio). The pincushion is stuffed with fiberfill and has a little sandbag inside to weight it. This is a great project for using up some of your small scraps. I hope you'll get creative and make it a home of your own!

Materials and Supplies

FABRIC SCRAPS: At least 9 contrasting scraps 5″ square or larger for cabin walls, roof, windows, doors, tree, and needle book*

WOOL FELT: 4″ square or larger scrap for needle book

MUSLIN: 3½″ × 7″ or larger scrap for sandbag

WOVEN COTTON FUSIBLE INTERFACING: 1 fat quarter

POLYESTER FIBERFILL

BUTTON: for needle book

SAND OR LIZARD LITTER: to fill 3″ square flat sandbag

APPLIQUÉ GLUE

THREAD: to contrast with color of doors and windows and with cabin front

The windows and doors should be different from the walls, and it's nice if the roof contrasts as well.

Cutting

Use the patterns (page 32) for the tree and the roof sides.

CABIN FRONT AND BACK WALLS: Cut 2 pieces 5″ × 4″ *each* from fabric and interfacing.

CABIN SIDE WALLS: Cut 2 pieces 3½″ × 4″ *each* from fabric and interfacing.

ROOF FRONT AND BACK: Cut 2 pieces 5″ × 3″ *each* from fabric and interfacing.

ROOF SIDES: Cut 2 pattern A pieces *each* from fabric and interfacing.

CABIN BOTTOM: Cut 1 piece 5″ × 3½″ *each* from fabric and interfacing.

DOOR APPLIQUÉ: Cut 1 piece 1″ × 2″ from fabric.

WINDOW APPLIQUÉS: Cut 10 squares 1″ × 1″.

TREE APPLIQUÉ: Cut 1 pattern B piece from fabric.

NEEDLE BOOK:

Cut 1 piece 3½″ × 2½″ *each* from fabric and wool felt, using pinking shears to cut both at once with wrong sides together.

Cut 1 strip 1″ × 2″ from fabric for button loop.

SANDBAG: Cut 2 squares 3½″ × 3½″ from muslin.

Construction

MAKE THE CABIN WALLS

To prevent fraying and stabilize the fabric for quilting, press the interfacing pieces to the wrong sides of the wall, roof, and bottom pieces before you start sewing.

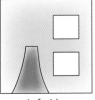
Left side

Front side

Right side

Cabin front

NOTE: Position the front and back panels with the 5″ edges at the top and bottom.

1. Referring to the photo, use appliqué glue to adhere the windows and doors to the front panel.

2. Using your free-motion quilting foot and with the feed dogs down, sew on the door and windows. Using this method, you can simply doodle with your thread. Create window frame and door details, and add a scalloped edge ½″ from the top for an artful roofline.

Cabin back with needle book

1. To make the button loop, press each long edge of the 1″ × 2″ fabric strip under ¼″, then fold in half lengthwise with wrong sides together. Edgestitch the open edges together.

2. Layer the felt and cotton needle book fabrics with wrong sides together. Fold in half to form a book with the felt on the inside. Mark the center fold at the top and bottom with pins.

3. Fold the button loop in half and tack the ends together with glue. With the felt side of the book facing up, insert the loop ends between the layers in the center of the left edge. Beginning and ending at the center pin marks, topstitch around the left-hand side of the book, catching the loop ends in the stitching.

4. Fold the book in half again and center it on the cabin back. Beginning and ending at the center pins, topstitch the right-hand side of the book to the cabin back. Sew a button onto the cabin back to correspond with the loop for fastening the book closed.

Cabin sides

NOTE: Position the cabin sides with the 3½″ edges at the top and bottom.

1. For the right-hand side of the cabin (when viewed from the front), glue windows in place and free-motion quilt as you did on the cabin front.

2. For the left-hand side of the cabin, glue and then free-motion quilt the tree trunk and the windows in place. Use green thread to add a mass of stitching for tree leaves. Then free-motion stitch with contrasting thread on top.

ASSEMBLE THE CABIN

Front, back, and sides

1. Mark a small dot ¼″ from each corner on the wrong side of all pieces. Use these dots as starting and ending points for each of your seams, and backstitch at each end.

2. Sew the top edges of the cabin front and cabin back pieces to the bottom edges of the roof pieces. Press the seams up. Sew the front and back together at the roof and press the seam to one side.

3. Sew the top edge of each cabin side to the bottom edge of 1 roof side piece A. Press the seams down.

NOTE: This is the opposite direction from the way you pressed the front and back seams. This is so you can easily sew the side to the front layer by nesting the seams.

4. With right sides together, align 1 side panel (cabin side and pattern A) to the front roof / wall panel that you constructed earlier. Nest the seams together. Sew the roof sides to the roof fronts and backs. Repeat for the remaining side.

5. Sew the front and back walls to the side walls. Press.

Sandbag

On such a large pincushion, you'll need something to weight the bottom down so it won't tilt. For this reason, I have you construct a sandbag.

1. Sew the muslin squares together, leaving a 1½″ opening to fill with sand.

2. Fill with sand or lizard litter and hand stitch the opening closed.

BARI J. ACKERMAN is a product and textile designer whose work has been featured in such publications as *Sew Somerset*, *Romantic Homes*, *Haute Handbags*, and many more. She lives in Scottsdale, Arizona.

WEBSITE: barijdesigns.com

This project originally appeared in *Inspired to Sew by Bari J.* by Bari J. Ackerman, available from Stash Books.

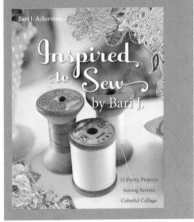

FINISH AND STUFF THE CABIN

1. Sew the bottom piece to 3 sides of the cabin, beginning and ending at the marked dots.

2. Turn the cabin right side out. Press the open bottom edges under ¼″.

3. Stuff the cabin firmly with fiberfill, and when it's nice and full, place the sandbag inside at the bottom. Before you close the seam, check to see if the house stands up straight. You will probably have to fiddle around with the placement of the sandbag to get it just right.

4. Hand stitch the opening closed using a blind stitch.

Ladybug Pincushion

Julie M. Creus

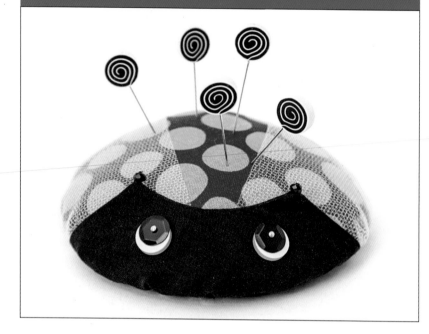

FINISHED SIZE:
4" diameter × 1¼" tall

Tulle wings and layered buttons give a wide-eyed, cartoony look to this whimsical pincushion.

JULIE CREUS has been dubbed by friends as "La Todera," mistress of all trades. She designs fabrics, teaches craft classes, and creates unique, stylish items with clever construction methods. She lives in Orlando, Florida.

WEBSITE: latodera.com

This project originally appeared in *Adventures in Fabric—La Todera Style* by Julie M. Creus, available from Stash Books.

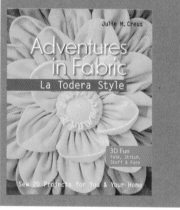

Materials and Cutting

Use ladybug patterns A–E (pages 27 and 28) to cut your pieces.

Fabric	For	Cutting
7" × 7" square of polka dot	Body	Cut 1 piece using pattern C.
7" × 7" square of black solid	Head	See Construction, Body, Step 1 (next page), for pattern A directions.
7" × 14" white tulle	Wings	Cut 2 pieces using pattern B.
Felt scrap at least 4" × 4" square	Base	Use pinking shears to cut 1 piece using pattern E.

Findings: Stuffing, 4" round chipboard coaster (or cardboard trimmed into a 4" circle using pattern D), extra-strong thread, 2 white buttons ⅓" wide, 2 black sequins ¼" wide, 2 black beads, 2 straight pins

Tools: Clear template plastic, fabric marker, pinking shears, scissors, turning tool, hot-glue gun, white glue

Construction

BODY

1. Fold the 7″ × 7″ black fabric in half, right sides together. Trace pattern A (page 28) onto the fabric. Sew directly on the pattern's dotted line. With pinking shears, trim the seam allowance to ¼″; trim the corners straight across. Use scissors to cut directly on the remaining lines. Turn right side out and push the corners out.

2. Place the polka dot body circle right side up. Lay the folded tulle fabric pieces on top of the circle. Match the raw edges of tulle to the raw edges of the body fabric, with the top corners of tulle touching. Place the black headpiece on top of the body fabric and tulle, centering it where the tulle meets. Pin.

3. Thread a needle with 24″ extra-strong thread and knot the end. Backstitch at the bottom of the assembled pieces, then stitch around the perimeter, using a ¼″ stitch length and seam allowance. Do not backstitch or cut the thread.

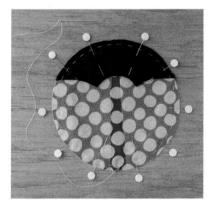

4. With the assembled ladybug face-down, place stuffing onto the center of the circle. Place a coaster onto the stuffing. Draw the thread to pull the fabric around the coaster about ½″, compressing the stuffing. Backstitch, knot, and trim the thread.

5. Hot-glue felt to the bottom to cover the coaster and raw edges.

FACE

1. Thread 2 straight pins with a black seed bead. Apply a bit of white glue to the pin shaft. Insert into the points of black fabric.

2. Thread 2 straight pins with a black sequin, then a button. Audition the eye placement, then pull the pins out slightly, add a bit of white glue under the buttons, and push back in place. Let dry.

Elephant Sewing Caddy

Jill Hamor

FINISHED SIZE: 5″ tall

Based on a vintage pattern from the 1920s, this full sewing caddy, complete with pincushion, would make a practical, playful gift.

JILL HAMOR, a Southern California native, received degrees from both UCLA and UC Berkeley, before diving head-first into the world of handcrafting. She was inspired to design, sew, and knit by her own kids, nieces, and nephews. Jill resides in the San Francisco Bay Area.

WEBSITE: bybido.blogspot.com

This project originally appeared in *Storybook Toys* by Jill Hamor, available from Stash Books.

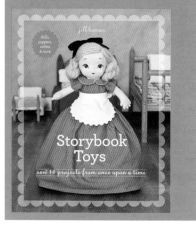

Materials and Supplies

WOOL FELT:

2 pieces 8″ × 12″ for body, legs, and ears

Scraps for hat, pincushion, and accessories

STUFFING

EMBROIDERY FLOSS for eyes and blanket

STRAWBERRY EMERY clipped off a tomato pincushion for tail (*optional*)

DOLL NEEDLE

4½″ BUTTONS to secure legs

THIMBLE for trunk (*optional*)

Construction

Trace the patterns (pages 29 and 30) onto freezer paper and press them onto the felt. Cut out the pieces before removing the freezer-paper templates.

All seams are stitched wrong sides together, leaving seam allowances on the outside, unless otherwise noted.

BODY

1. Fold the darts right sides together and sew them on the elephant side body and head gusset pieces using a small whipstitch.

2. With the darts facing the inside of the body, match A to B and sew the

trunk gusset to a side of the body. Repeat for the other side.

3. With the darts still facing the inside of the body, align the dart of a center head gusset with the upper dart on the side head and whipstitch from the back of the head toward the front of the center head gusset. Repeat for the other side and continue to whipstitch to the end of the trunk.

4. Sew the back together from the back of the head gusset to the back darts.

5. Match C to D and align the underbody gusset in place, positioning the underbody gusset on the *outside* of the trunk gusset. Sew each side. The underbody gusset will overlap the trunk and is wider at the mouth, so the mouth of the elephant will appear to be open.

6. Stuff the elephant's head and then the body. Use the palm of your hand to cradle and shape the elephant's head as you stuff it firmly. Finish stuffing and sewing the body.

7. Place the 2 short ends of the trunk lining together and whipstitch. Insert the trunk lining inside the trunk opening, test the fit with a thimble (placed inside the trunk opening), and adjust if necessary. Whipstitch around the upper edge of the trunk opening.

EARS AND LEGS

1. Place 2 ear pieces together and sew around the outer edge. Repeat for the other 2 ear pieces. Place the ears on the head, covering the upper head dart, and sew them securely in place.

2. Place 2 leg pieces together and sew from the bottom of a side to the bottom of the other side.

3. Place the circular foot pad in place and sew to the bottom of the leg. Stuff the leg as you go until the foot pad is sewn on and the leg is sewn closed. Repeat for the remaining 3 legs.

4. Secure the legs to the elephant's sides using buttons and a doll needle to sew back and forth through the elephant's body, anchoring the front legs first and then the back legs.

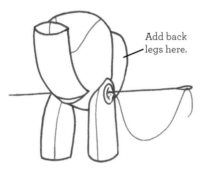

Add back legs here.

ELEPHANT DETAILS

1. Use pinking shears to trim the circular edge of the hat and then sew the straight edges of the hat together. Turn the seam to the inside and turn up the brim of the hat. Add stuffing and secure the hat to the top of the elephant's head.

2. Pink the edges of the smaller blanket and sew it to the larger blanket with a running stitch. Add the rectangular piece to a side of the blanket to hold tiny scissors. Take a few stitches on each of the short sides of the blanket to secure it in place.

3. Fold the tail in half and whipstitch along the length. As you approach the curve, whipstitch the tail in place on the elephant's backside.

4. *Optional:* Sew the strawberry top to the strawberry and then whipstitch the bottom of the tail to the strawberry.

5. Embroider the elephant's eyes using small pieces of black wool felt and stitches with black embroidery floss.

PINCUSHION

1. Sew the triangles to the pincushion strip.

2. Sew the stars to the pincushion strip.

3. Sew the short ends of the strip together to form a ring.

4. Blanket stitch the strip to the circular top and bottom bases; stuff while closing.

Picnic Ant Pincushion

Susan Maw and Sally Bell

FINISHED SIZE: 7″ × 2½″

These giant ants may cause some concern at your next picnic! But don't worry—they will only take the leftovers for themselves.

Designed and made by Susan Maw

Photos in project by Jesse Maw

SUSAN MAW and **SALLY BELL** are sisters, long-time collaborators, and partners in Maw Bell Designs, specializing in patterns for quilts, children's clothing, and accessories. Susan lives in Kalispell, Montana, near Glacier National Park, and Sally lives in the state's Bitterroot Valley.

WEBSITE: maw-belldesigns.com

Materials and Supplies

ANT BODY/HEAD: 1 fat eighth

2 BUTTONS ¼″ OR BEADS for eyes

BEADS for antennae

16-GAUGE WIRE 33″ for legs (Wire can be purchased at a craft store.)

20-GAUGE WIRE 8″ for antennae

STUFFING

CRAFT GLUE

WIRE CUTTERS

NEEDLE-NOSE PLIERS

Cutting

Use the patterns (page 32) to cut the ant body and head pieces.

Cut 3 ant bodies.

Cut 3 ant heads.

Cut 3 pieces 11″ of 16-gauge wire for legs.

Cut 2 pieces 4″ of 20-gauge wire for antennae.

Construction

A ¼″ seam allowance is included in the templates.

1. With right sides together, sew 2 ant bodies from straight end to dot, back-stitching at the beginning and end. Pin this to the third body piece, matching the dots. Stitch from straight end to dot, backstitching at both ends. Clip the curves and turn the body right side out.

2. Repeat Step 1 with the ant head pieces.

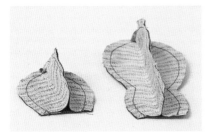

3. Stuff the body and head firmly.

4. Finger-press the seam allowances under. Pin the head to the body, matching the body seams to the centers of the head pieces. Hand stitch them together. A body seam and flat side of the head are the top of the ant.

5. Sew a button eye to each side of the head. Pass the needle through 1 button, back through the head, and through the second button. Pull the thread slightly as you sew to indent the buttons.

6. Place the center of a wire leg at the bottom of the neck seam. With your fingers, bring the end of the wire around to the top and twist it once (180°) to indent the body. Use needle-nose pliers to twist the ends of the wire into a coil.

7. Repeat Step 6 with the remaining 2 wire legs, placing one at the indent in the body and the other in the center of the first 2 wires. Bend the wires down about ½″ out from the body. Level the ant by adjusting the bends. The back end of the ant body should touch the flat surface.

8. Twist one end of each antenna wire into a coil. Add the beads. Put a dab of glue on the straight end of the wires and push them into the top of the head. Bend the wires slightly forward.

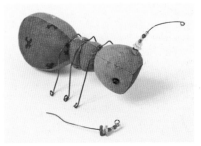

Hot Fudge Sundae Pincushion

Jessica Peck

FINISHED SIZE:
3¼" high × 3¼" in diameter

Ice cream is always a special treat. Being able to enjoy it while you sew—without the mess—is just the cherry on top!

Designed by Jessica Peck; made by Sarah Frost

JESSICA PECK, a graduate of Harrington College of Design, creates all her designs on the playroom floor. From conception to completion, her children inspire her creativity. She also designs a line of sewing patterns called Sweetie Pie Bakery. She lives in Wisconsin with her family.

WEBSITE: jessicapeck.blogspot.com

This project originally appeared in *Felt Toys for Little Ones* by Jessica Peck, available from Stash Books.

Materials and Supplies

Use the patterns (page 31) to trace and cut the sundae pieces.

Material	Amount	Cut
White felt	9″ × 12″	Cut 1 whipped cream (D), 1 scoop of ice cream top (B), and 2 scoop of ice cream bases (A).
Gray felt	9″ × 12″	Cut 14 cup sides (A) and 2 cup bottoms (B).
Brown felt	5″ × 5″	Cut 1 hot fudge (C).
Red felt	3″ × 3″	Cut 1 cherry (E).
Tan felt	3″ × 3″	Cut ⅛″ × ⅛″ squares for chopped nuts.
Ivory felt	3″ × 3″	Cut ⅛″ × ⅛″ squares for chopped nuts.
fast2fuse heavy double-sided stiff fusible interfacing	8″ × 8″	Cut 7 cup side supports (A1) and 1 cup bottom support (B1).
Embroidery floss—gray, white, brown, red, tan		
Stuffing		

Construction

SCOOP

1. Place 2 scoop bases (A) right sides together. Sew around the perimeter by machine, leaving an opening to turn right side out.

2. Turn the scoop base (A) right side out. Stuff the scoop base (A) and blind-stitch the opening closed. Set aside.

3. With the wrong side up, run a basting stitch around the scoop top (B).

4. Begin to add stuffing as you pull the thread taut on the scoop top (B). Tie a knot to secure the thread once the scoop top (B) is fully stuffed.

5. Place the scoop top (B) over the scoop base (A). Blindstitch around the base of the scoop top (B) to secure it to the scoop base (A). Set aside.

Blind stitch.

SUNDAE

1. Following the manufacturer's instructions, fuse a cup side support (A1) to the wrong side of a cup side (A). Repeat with remaining 6 cup side supports. Fuse cup bottom support (B1) to wrong side of cup bottom (B).

2. Fuse a plain cup side (A) to an interfaced cup side (A), wrong sides together. Repeat with remaining 6 cup side (A) pairs. Fuse the plain cup bottom (B) to the interfaced cup bottom (B), wrong sides together. Set aside.

3. Place 2 fused cup sides (A) together, and stitch together along 1 side using a blanket stitch.

4. Continue adding remaining fused cup sides (A) until you have connected 7 sides and formed a cup shape.

5. Use a blanket stitch to attach the fused cup bottom (B) to the attached cup sides (A). Blanket stitch along top edges of cup.

Blanket stitch.

6. Use a blanket stitch to attach the hot fudge (C) to the top of the scoop of ice cream you had set aside.

7. Make small stitches to attach the small tan and ivory felt squares (nuts) on top of the hot fudge (C).

8. To make a whipped cream dollop, prepare a needle with 2 strands of floss and a knot at the base of the thread. With the whipped cream (D) *wrong side up*, take the needle down and up through a felt tip just to catch the thread. Pull the thread all the way through to catch the knot.

9. Moving counterclockwise, take the needle through the next felt tip, going in from the right side and out through the wrong side. Continue this process all the way around the whipped cream (D).

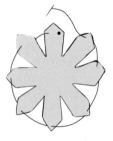

10. Pull the thread taut, gathering the whipped cream (D) into a neat little dollop. Secure the thread with a knot to complete the whipped cream. Use a blind stitch to attach the whipped cream to the top of the hot fudge (C).

11. To create the cherry (E), sew a gathering stitch around the perimeter of the cherry (E), with the wrong side facing up.

12. As you begin to pull the thread taut, add stuffing to the cherry (E). After it is stuffed, tie a knot to secure.

13. For the stem, stitch 6 strands of embroidery floss through the top of the cherry (E). Holding the strands together, braid the floss together, and then tie a knot at the end.

14. Use a blind stitch to attach the cherry (E) to the top of the whipped cream (D).

Blind stitch.

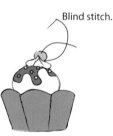

Three Pretty Pincushions

Leanne Beasley of Leanne's House

Quick and easy to complete, these are great projects to send to a friend across the miles; every time she stitches she'll think of you.

LEANNE BEASLEY is an artist who seeks to inspire other women to express their creativity. She produces *Vignette* magazine, which includes photography, drawings, and recipes, and her work has appeared in many magazines and books. Based out of Australia, Leanne also travels the world teaching, hosting travel retreats, and journaling her adventures.

WEBSITE: leanneshouse.com

This project originally appeared in *Stitch Zakka* (from Stash Books), which was compiled by Gailen Runge.

Materials and Supplies

EMBROIDERY HOOP (*optional*)

Sunshine Yellow Pincushion

YELLOW PRINT: 1 square 9" × 9" for front

GREEN PRINT: 1 square 9" × 9" for back

EMBROIDERY FLOSS: Yellow, pink, red, and green

THIN FUSIBLE BATTING: 2 squares 9" × 9"

YELLOW RICKRACK: ½ yard, ⅞" wide

STUFFING

Bonny Blue Pincushion

BLUE PRINT: 2 squares 9" × 9"

EMBROIDERY FLOSS: Yellow-green, light blue, medium blue, and aqua

THIN FUSIBLE BATTING: 2 squares 9" × 9"

JADE RICKRACK: ½ yard, ¾" wide

STUFFING

2 BUTTONS, ¾" in diameter

Perfect Pink Pincushion

PINK PRINT: 2 squares 11" × 11"

EMBROIDERY FLOSS: Pink, red, lime green, and orange

THIN FUSIBLE BATTING: 2 squares 11" × 11"

PINK RICKRACK: ⅝ yard, ⅞" wide

STUFFING

2 BUTTONS, 1" in diameter

Construction

All seam allowances are ¼", unless otherwise specified. Use 2 strands of floss for all embroidery.

Refer to Embroidery Stitches (next page) as needed.

EMBROIDERY

1. Enlarge and transfer the embroidery design (page 28) and the outermost circle onto the pincushion front fabric.

2. Iron the fusible batting onto the wrong side of the pincushion front and back fabrics, following the manufacturer's instructions.

3. Embroider the design onto the front through both layers.

4. Press with a warm iron on the back, using an appliqué pressing sheet or Silicone Release Paper (from C&T Publishing) on top of the fusible batting.

Sunshine Yellow

Backstitch the flower petals using red floss.

Stitch French knots in the flower centers using pink floss.

Backstitch the stems and leaves using green floss.

Stitch French knots in the background using yellow floss.

Bonny Blue

Backstitch the flower petals using medium blue floss.

Satin stitch the flower centers using light blue floss.

Backstitch the stems and satin stitch the leaves using aqua floss.

Stitch French knots in the background using yellow-green floss.

Perfect Pink

Backstitch the flower petals using pink floss.

Satin stitch the flower centers using orange floss.

Satin stitch the leaves and backstitch the center circle using lime green floss.

Stitch French knots between the flowers using red floss.

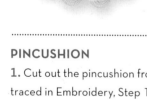 

PINCUSHION

1. Cut out the pincushion front on the cutting line circle traced in Embroidery, Step 1 (above).

2. Using the pincushion front as a guide, cut out the back from the coordinating piece of fabric.

3. On the right side of the pincushion front, pin and sew a piece of rickrack around the edge (using a ⅛" seam allowance), overlapping the ends and trimming the excess at the outside of the circle.

The side of the rickrack that faces into the circle when you pin will end up being the outside edge that is visible. Align the center of the rickrack about ¼" in from the edge of the circle.

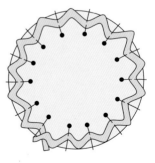

4. Place a matching pincushion front and back right sides together. Pin and stitch, leaving a small opening for turning and stuffing.

5. Clip the seam allowance all the way around between all the points of the rickrack; this is very important to prevent puckering. Turn right side out.

Clip.

6. Press lightly with a warm iron. Stuff. Hand stitch the opening closed through all the layers.

7. *Optional:* Stitch a button on the center top through all the layers. Once you have a few stitches holding the top button, add a button on the back in the same position. Stitch through both buttons a few times. When the buttons are secure, knot the floss close to the fabric behind the back button, pull the needle through the fabric and out again. Trim.

Embroidery Stitches

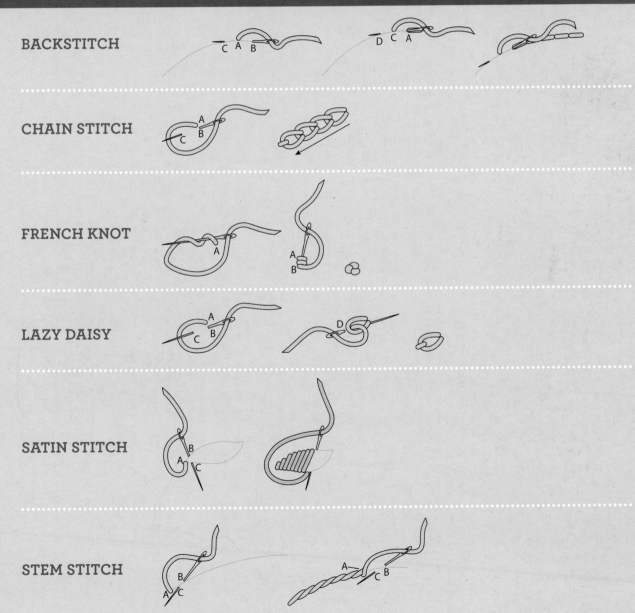

BACKSTITCH

CHAIN STITCH

FRENCH KNOT

LAZY DAISY

SATIN STITCH

STEM STITCH

New York Taxi Pincushion

Aneela Hoey

FINISHED SIZE: 4½″ × 3½″

This project makes a fun homemade souvenir of a bygone visit to the Big Apple.

ANEELA HOEY studied printed textile design and worked at design studios in both London and New York. She designs fabric lines for Moda Fabrics, as well as her own embroidery and quilt patterns. She was a co-founder of the popular online e-zine *Fat Quarterly* and writes the blog *ComfortStitching*. Aneela lives in Berkshire, England.

WEBSITE:
comfortstitching.typepad.co.uk

This project originally appeared in *Little Stitches* by Aneela Hoey, available from Stash Books.

Materials and Supplies

WHITE COTTON FABRIC: 8″ × 8″ piece of white cotton fabric

PRINT FABRIC: 4″ × 5″

BATTING: 4″ × 5″

STUFFING

5″ EMBROIDERY HOOP

EMBROIDERY FLOSS: yellow, gray, dark brown, red, orange

Construction

EMBROIDERY

Refer to Embroidery Stitches (page 23) as needed.

Transfer the taxi design (page 27) onto the center of the 8″ × 8″ white fabric and fix it in an embroidery hoop. Embroidery the design using the embroidery guide.

NEW YORK TAXI EMBROIDERY GUIDE

	Element	Color	# of strands	Stitch
Outline	Car	Yellow	6	Backstitch
	Windows	Gray	2	Backstitch
	Tires	Dark brown	6	Backstitch
	Inner tires	Dark brown	1	Backstitch
Outline and fill	Taillight	Red	6	Backstitch
Embroider	Road, door edge, taxi sign	Dark brown	1	Backstitch
	Headlight	Orange	6	Straight stitch
	Speed marks, door handles	Dark brown	1	Straight stitch

PINCUSHION

1. Remove the embroidery from the hoop and press, taking care not to iron the embroidered parts.

2. Cut the embroidered fabric down to 5″ × 4″, keeping the embroidery centered.

3. Place the embroidered fabric right side up on top of the batting and baste in place with a couple of stitches. Quilt a few random lines across the width above and below the embroidery.

4. Place the embroidered piece and the print fabric right sides together. Pin and baste the edges. Machine stitch all around the outside edge with a ¼″ seam allowance, leaving a 3″ gap at one end. Trim a little of the excess fabric from the corners to reduce bulk (but not too close to the stitching).

5. Turn right side out and fill the pincushion with the stuffing until plump.

6. Fold the raw edges of the opening in and hand sew the opening closed.

Fold raw edges inward.

Bunny Pincushion

Anne Sutton of Bunny Hill Designs

FINISHED SIZE: 6″ × 6″

This little bunny will hold your pins while you sew!

ANNE SUTTON is the owner and designer of Bunny Hill Designs. She specializes in appliqué and embroidery, often bringing her love of animals to her designs. In addition to her quilt patterns, Anne also designs fabric for Moda Fabrics. Find more of her work on her website and blog.

WEBSITE: bunnyhilldesigns.com

This project originally appeared in *Stitch Zakka* (from Stash Books), which was compiled by Gailen Runge.

Materials and Supplies

CREAM LINEN: 1 square 6½″ × 6½″

ASSORTED FABRICS: 2 pieces 1″ × 1½″ each of 5 prints for side borders

PRINT FABRIC: 2 strips 1″ × 6½″ for top and bottom borders

BACKING: 1 square 6½″ × 6½″

EMBROIDERY FLOSS: Brown, coral, pink, orange, green, light pink, light orange, and gray

STUFFING

Construction

EMBROIDERY

Refer to Embroidery Stitches (page 23) as needed.

1. Transfer the bunny design (below right) onto the linen using your favorite method.

2. Embroider the design using the embroidery guide.

PINCUSHION

All seam allowances are ¼".

1. Trim the embroidered square to 5½" × 5½".

2. Sew 5 of the 1" × 1½" assorted fabric pieces together at the short ends and press. Repeat with the remaining 5 pieces.

3. Sew the pieced borders to the sides of the embroidered square and press toward the borders.

4. Sew the print strips to the top and bottom of the embroidered square and press toward the borders.

5. With right sides together, stitch the pincushion front to the pincushion back, leaving a 2" opening at the center bottom and backstitching at the beginning and end.

6. Turn right side out and gently push out the corners. Fill the pincushion (I used ground walnut shells). Slipstitch the opening closed.

BUNNY EMBROIDERY GUIDE

Color	Element	# of strands	Stitch
Brown	Head, ears	3	Stem stitch
	Eye, nose	2	Satin stitch
	Whiskers	2	Straight stitch
	Mouth, paws	2	Backstitch
	Purse handle	3	Chain stitch
Coral	Dress	3	Stem stitch
	Collar, tie	2	Backstitch
Pink	Cup	3	Stem stitch
	Purse	2	Backstitch
	Flower centers (purse)	2	French knots
Orange	Flowers (cup)	2	Backstitch
Green	Leaves	2	Lazy daisy
Light pink	Inner ear	2	Backstitch
Light orange	Flowers (purse)	2	Lazy daisy
	Thread	3	Stem stitch
Gray	Needle	2	Straight stitch

Bunny Pincushion
(page 25)

Patterns

New York Taxi Pincushion

(page 24)

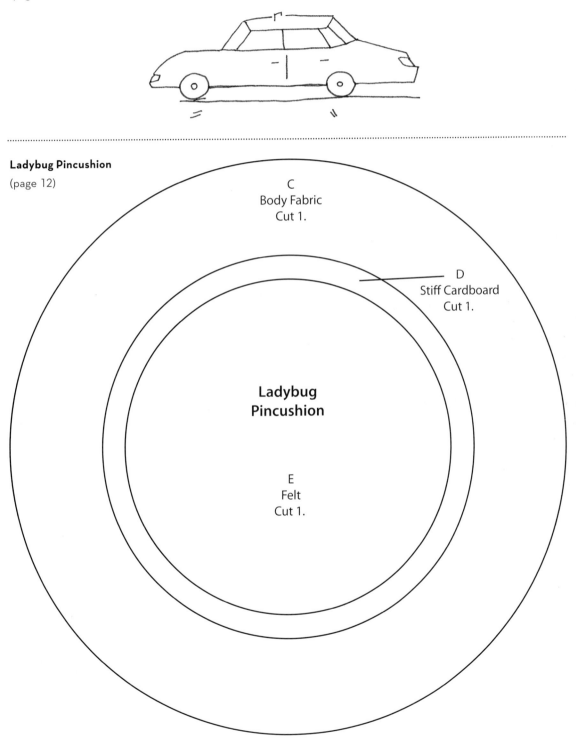

Ladybug Pincushion

(page 12)

C
Body Fabric
Cut 1.

D
Stiff Cardboard
Cut 1.

**Ladybug
Pincushion**

E
Felt
Cut 1.

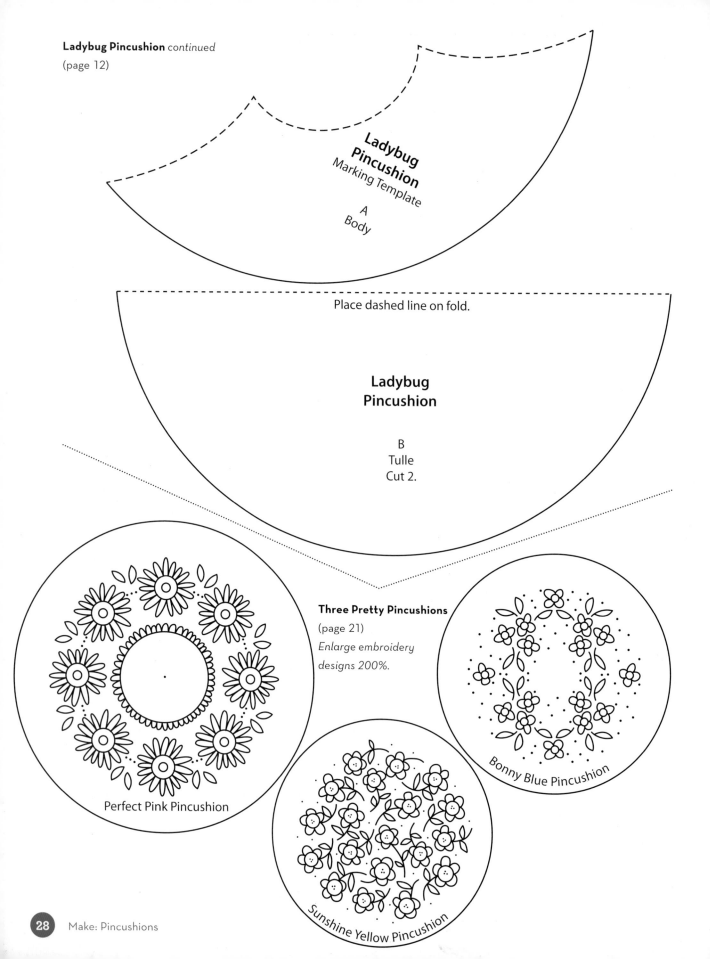

Ladybug
Pincushion
Marking Template

A
Body

Place dashed line on fold.

Ladybug
Pincushion

B
Tulle
Cut 2.

Three Pretty Pincushions
(page 21)
*Enlarge embroidery
designs 200%.*

Perfect Pink Pincushion

Bonny Blue Pincushion

Sunshine Yellow Pincushion

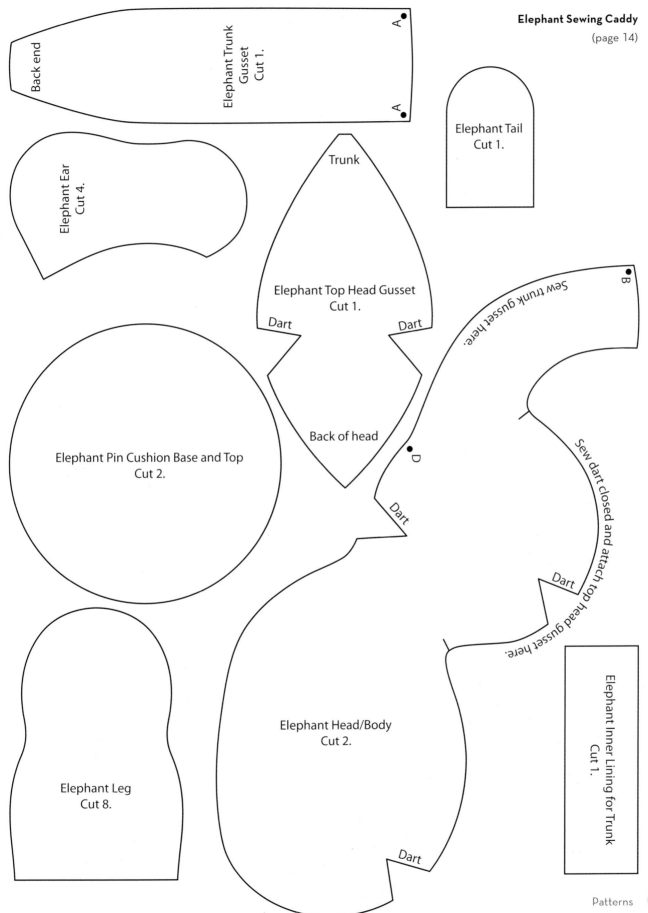

Back end

Elephant Trunk Gusset
Cut 1.

A

A

Elephant Tail
Cut 1.

Elephant Ear
Cut 4.

Trunk

Elephant Top Head Gusset
Cut 1.

Dart

Dart

Sew trunk gusset here.

B

Back of head

D

Dart

Sew dart closed and attach top head gusset here.

Dart

Elephant Pin Cushion Base and Top
Cut 2.

Elephant Head/Body
Cut 2.

Elephant Inner Lining for Trunk
Cut 1.

Elephant Leg
Cut 8.

Dart

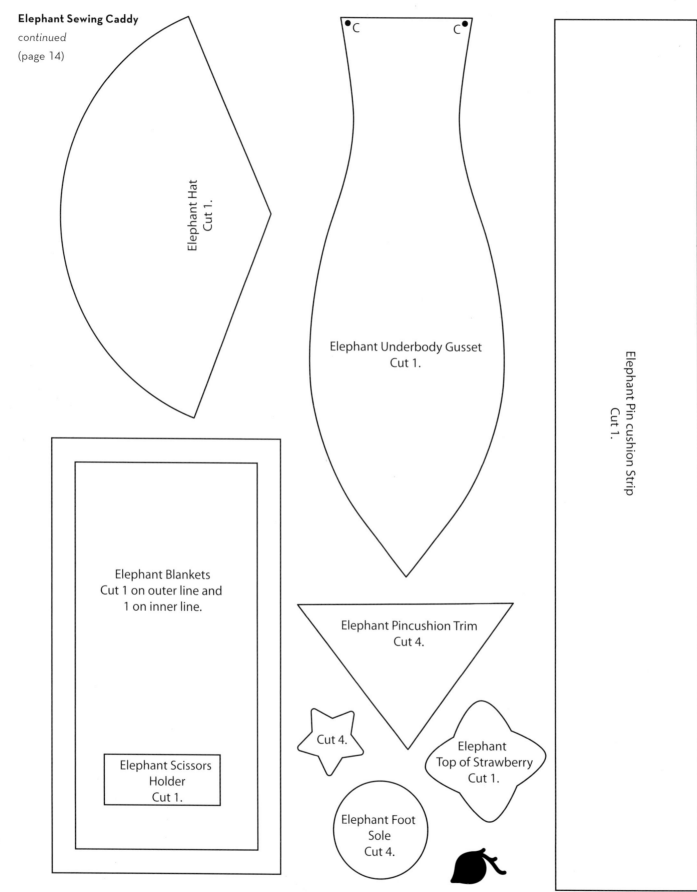

Elephant Hat
Cut 1.

C   C

Elephant Underbody Gusset
Cut 1.

Elephant Pin cushion Strip
Cut 1.

Elephant Blankets
Cut 1 on outer line and
1 on inner line.

Elephant Scissors
Holder
Cut 1.

Elephant Pincushion Trim
Cut 4.

Cut 4.

Elephant
Top of Strawberry
Cut 1.

Elephant Foot
Sole
Cut 4.

Elephant Eye

Hot Fudge Sundae Pincushion

(page 18)

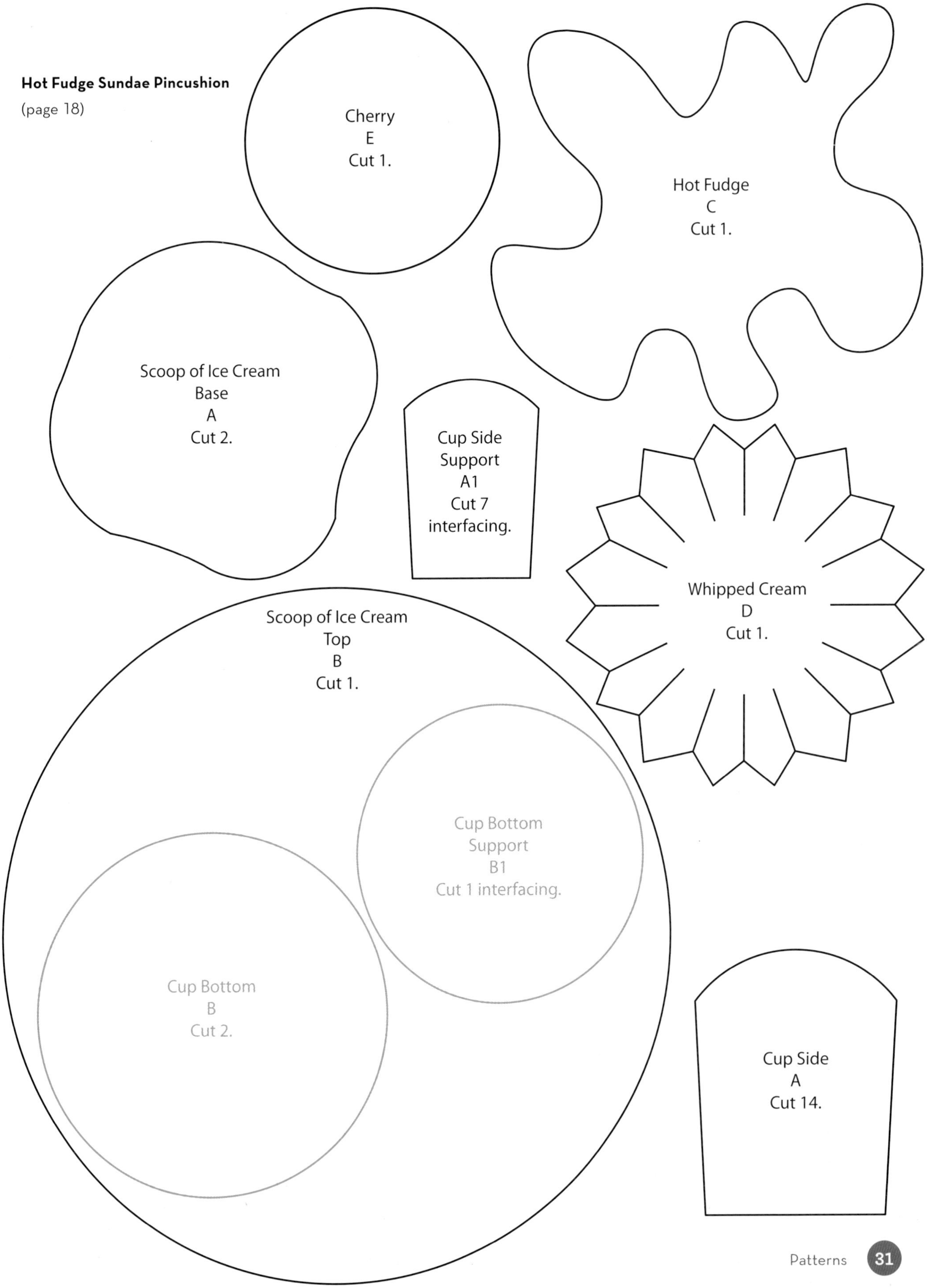

Cherry
E
Cut 1.

Hot Fudge
C
Cut 1.

Scoop of Ice Cream
Base
A
Cut 2.

Cup Side
Support
A1
Cut 7
interfacing.

Whipped Cream
D
Cut 1.

Scoop of Ice Cream
Top
B
Cut 1.

Cup Bottom
Support
B1
Cut 1 interfacing.

Cup Bottom
B
Cut 2.

Cup Side
A
Cut 14.

Picnic Ant Pincushion

(page 16)

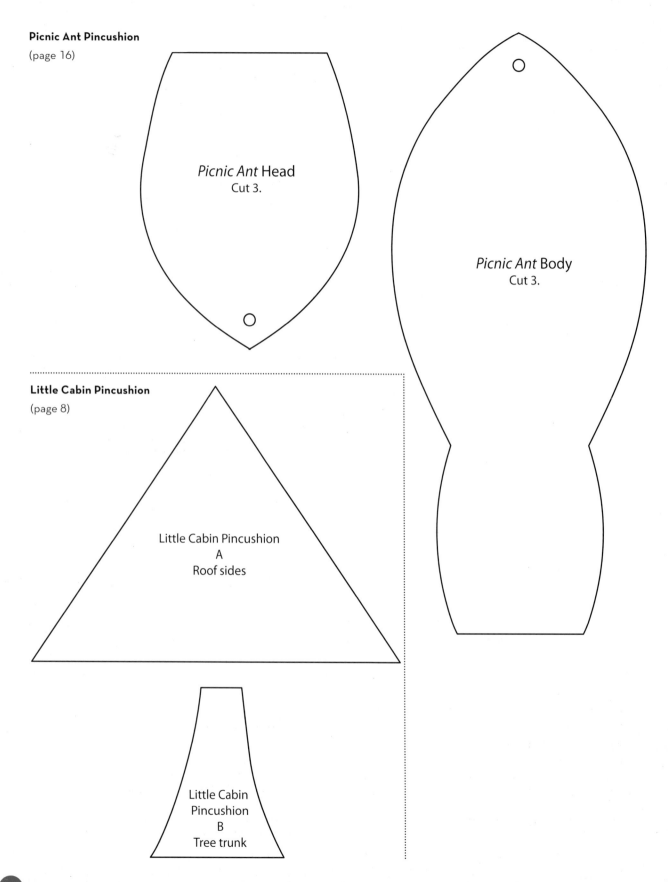

Picnic Ant Head
Cut 3.

Picnic Ant Body
Cut 3.

Little Cabin Pincushion

(page 8)

Little Cabin Pincushion
A
Roof sides

Little Cabin
Pincushion
B
Tree trunk